THAT DOG MELLY!

by CORINNE DEMAS BLISS
with AUSTIN BLISS

Photographs by

Corinne Demas Bliss

and Jim Judkis

HASTINGS HOUSE
PUBLISHERS
New York 10016

Library of Congress Cataloging in Publication Data

Bliss, Corinne Demas.   That dog Melly!

   Summary: A six-year-old's runaway dog sits tantalizingly out of
reach across a street the child is not permitted to cross.
   [1. Dogs—Fiction]   I. Bliss, Austin, joint author.
II. Judkis, Jim.   III. Title.
PZ7.B61917Th 1980   [E]   80-36701
ISBN 0-8038-7217-8

Published simultaneously in Canada by Saunders of Toronto, Ltd.,
Don Mills, Ontario

Printed in the United States of America

PICTURE CREDITS: Corinne Demas Bliss, pages 3–5, 10–16, 18–19,
20–21, 21 bottom, 22, 23 right, 25–27, 29–32; Jim Judkis,
1, 6, 7, 9, 17, 20 left, 23 left, 24, 28.

My dog's name is Melly, but nobody says it right.
Lots of people call her "Nelly" by mistake.
She doesn't mind.
She comes if you call her "Jelly" or "Belly."
Sometimes I even call her "Smelly" and she comes
running over and just smiles and wags her tail.

My mommy got Melly
before she got me.
When I was born,
Melly wasn't a puppy anymore.
She was already a dog.
I have pictures of Melly
when she was a puppy.
She was smaller than I was
when I was a baby.

Now I can't even pick her up.

Sometimes Melly is a lot more like a person than a dog.

She likes to watch my electric trains.

When I go to school in the morning
Melly always watches me leave.
She naps while I'm gone.

When I get home she wakes up and starts barking.
She always barks when she hears a noise
just in case it's a burglar
so she'll frighten him away.

When she sees it's only me, she jumps up and down
and licks my nose.
She always wants to see if I have anything
left over from lunch.

It's my job to feed Melly.
Every night I give her three cups of dog food
and all the supper I didn't eat.
When I forget, she kicks the bowl around and makes noise.
Melly likes the kind of food people eat.
String beans, bananas, and spaghetti.

She loves apples and she even eats the parts you
aren't supposed to eat—the stem and the seeds.
If you leave an apple on the table . . .

. . . and it disappears when you're gone . . .

. . . it's Melly!

We have a big yard for Melly and me to play in.
There's a fence all around so she won't run away.
But what she loves best is to go for walks.

She likes to sniff around
where other dogs have been.
If she sees a squirrel I have to hold on to her leash
with both hands till the squirrel runs up a tree.

Melly's so strong!
When I was a baby my mommy would
tie Melly to my carriage
and she would pull me up all the hills.

One day I took my stuffed animals out in my wagon
so Melly could pull them around.
But I didn't see her anywhere.
"Melly," I called. "Melly!"
But she didn't come.

So I yelled louder, "Melly, come!"
But she didn't come.
Then I tried to whistle.
But I don't know how to really whistle yet.

I looked all over the yard.
I didn't see her anywhere.

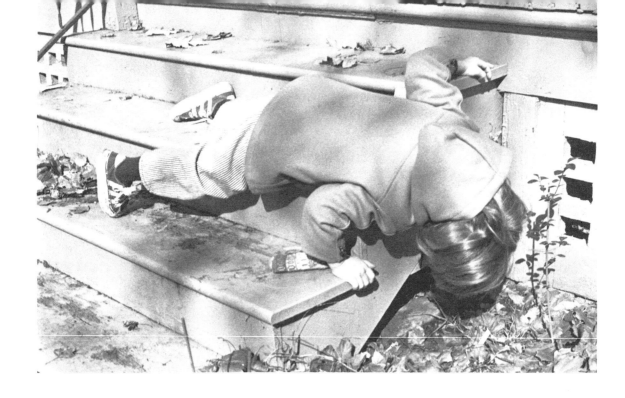

She wasn't under the back stairs.
And she wasn't behind the tree.

And she wasn't under the bush
where our secret hide-out is.

Then I saw something terrible.
Somebody had left the gate open!

I ran out in front of the house
and looked up and down the street.
Melly wasn't there.

I ran down the block and looked
around the corner.
No Melly.

Then I saw this big kid who lives near us.
I told her I was looking for my dog.
"Is she the one that's big and sort of fluffy
and dirty looking?" she asked.
I said yes.
She pointed towards my house,
"I saw her headed that way."

I started back towards my house
and then I saw her.
Soon as I got close, she took off.
I went after her.
I ran
and ran
but Melly was faster.

I chased her around the whole block.
She slowed down near our house
and I almost got her
but then she ran across the street.
I'm not allowed to cross the street.
All I could do was try and call her back.

"Melly! Mel-ly!"
She just sat there across the street.
And she wouldn't come.
"Melly!"
I called and called.
But she still wouldn't come.

She made me so mad I started to cry.
I sat down and tried to think about
what to do.
Then I had an idea.
I went inside and got Melly's leash.
I stood at the corner and jiggled the leash
so the chain part made noise.
Melly stood up.
"Want to go for a walk?" I shouted.
"I'm going for a walk!"

That Melly! Do you know what that silly dog did?
Just what I thought—
She came running across the street!

I just turned around and walked away
and sure enough, Melly followed right behind me!

When she was really close, I stopped.
"Want to go for a walk?" I said.
Melly wagged her tail and sat right down
so I could put on her leash.

I promised Melly a walk, so I gave her a walk.
We went all the way around the block
and back home again,
up the front steps and right through the gate and
into our back yard. I closed the gate tight as I could
behind me. Then we walked around the house
and right in the back door.

And that's how I got Melly home again
when she ran away.